An Upward Spiral Grief Workbook And Journal

In Loving Memory of Linda L. Casebier

And when you leave here

which you will,

the endless skies will be lit

by the very light

you gave away.

For nothing of the heart

that is given is ever lost.

From the earth to eternity

it travels,

waiting way beyond the

stars to welcome you

back home.

By Christopher J. Manning

Introduction

I hope you find this workbook to be helpful. They say that time heals, but it's what you do with the time that matters. Try your best to express details of how you are feeling when completing the book. Instead of saying, I am sad, write in deeper detail of what that means to you and why. Then write about how you were able to deal with those feelings in that moment. The end of the book is dedicated to journaling. I strongly suggest you start writing, it can even be addressed to your loved one. This book was written in the same manner that I use to coach the bereaved. Grief doesn't have to last forever although your love will never cease.

Please let me know what you think of the book and leave a review. If you are interested in having me coach you through your journey, please contact me through the website www.upwardspiralgriefcoaching.com.

Table of Contents

Chapter 1.

What is grief

Before we delve into healing from grief, we need to know what it is. Grief is the natural response to loss. It is universal and several creatures in the wild have been studied and found to grieve, from whales to birds. The response is without rules. We go through several emotional stages to physical symptoms. It scars our soul. The moment when we see or hear that a very important person in our lives is gone our hearts are shattered and our minds are trying to comprehend the magnitude of what it means. Our lives will never be the same. We won't be able to hear their voice, look into their eyes, see their smiles or feel their embrace again. How can we ever be the same? Grief can easily be described as the worst pain of emotional suffering that a person can endure.

After working in deathcare as a Funeral Director and Embalmer, I have seen every type of death and relationship gone. Parents losing children, spouses losing their soulmate, grandparents leaving behind a heritage of family members, children losing their parents. I've also seen every kind of death, natural, suicide, homicide, and accidents. Some say loss is loss but that just isn't true. No one's story can be directly experienced the exact same way as another's. Grief is as unique as the one who we lost. Just as the depth of love cannot be measured, neither can the grief. However, as profound grief is as a response, it does not have to be for the rest of your life. More on that to come.

Mourning is the outward expression of loss. Crying, yelling, hiding from life, wearing black. The physical symptoms can be overwhelming, stomach pain, diarrhea, inability to sleep or sleeping too much, changes in diet, concentration is gone, excessive crying or numbness to emotion.

Grief can affect your entire mind, body, and spirit. As my grandmother would say," death isn't for the faint of heart but that's where it gets you."

Chapter 2.

Restaging the stages of grief

Many may be familiar with the 5 stages of grief by Elisabeth Kubler Ross. They were intended for the dying and anticipatory grief, although many apply them after a death. After a lot of thought and reflection on what I have witnessed and felt in my own time of loss, I came up with these stages: disbelief, regret, resentment, temper/frustration, detachment, sorrow, realization, awakening and gratitude. These are not in a particular order and you may not go through all of these emotions or you might jump from one to another. However, don't feel like there's a set back if you experience them more than once.

Chapter 3.

Disbelief

Whether you are there to see them take their last breath or not, you still cannot fathom it has happened. Some people, like me, need to see it to believe it. Although there may be situations that prevent you from being able to see your loved one. Months later you can find yourself shaking your head and saying, I just can't believe this has happened. Another thing that tends to be prevalent is the manner that the death occurred. You replay the event over and over again like a recording loop. I tell people that this is a trauma loop. When you go back and think about the final moments, you are trying to make sense of the now. In other words, I am sad because mom died, mom died because she was bleeding nonstop because she had cancer. We rewind to what took their life and what caused them to stop breathing. This might also be a place that you physically go to. A young man could have been killed in a car accident and his father often goes to the mile marker to figure out how it happened. These are examples of disbelief.

What thoughts were difficult for you to believe? How were you able to come to terms with them?

_____

_____

_____

_____

_____

_____

_____

_____

_____

_____

_____

_____

_____

_____

Chapter 4.

Regret

Regret can be when you second guess how you handled end of life decisions for your loved one. It is also regret that future plans will never come to fruition. Not saying everything you wanted to say. It's the would have, could have, should have statements that replay over and over again in our minds. These regrets can be very heavy in our thoughts and hurt us so much. However, we must understand that we cannot go back and believe that we made the right decision at the time based on the information that we were given. We act with positive intentions all the time and it's important to give yourself a break. You acted upon your given choices and chances are that anyone else would have done that same exact thing.

Do you have regrets? What could you have done differently and was it even possible to have done it differently?

_____

_____

_____

_____

_____

_____

_____

_____

_____

_____

_____

_____

_____

_____

_____

_____

_____

_____

Chapter 5.

Resentment

Resentment is having anger directed at others for decisions they made. You may have resentment towards the first responders, other family members or yourself for the way things were handled. Whether it was when your loved one immediately needed emergent help or maybe the funeral decisions. Resentment is a part of grief. Perhaps it's lack of care in the final moments where neglect and pain took place. Regardless of the circumstances, this burdening emotion eventually needs to be let go of, forgiveness in your heart will help reduce resentment.

Does someone deserve your forgiveness? Have you been able to let go of resentment? What did you do to resolve this?

_____

_____

_____

_____

_____

_____

_____

_____

_____

_____

_____

_____

_____

_____

_____

_____

_____

Chapter 6.

Temper /Frustration

You may find yourself losing your temper and being frustrated with people after a death. It often happens when you are trying to close out the financial details of someone's life. If you have to return to work a few days later, you may be a little snippy with your colleagues. This can stem from frustration that your loved one is not here anymore to help you. Maybe they died suddenly, and you are blindly trying to piece together what they had or didn't have and it's causing you a lot of stress. You might have to be both parents if you lost your spouse and have children. You might have to take care of a parent now. Your entire world can be affected in so many ways. It is natural to lose it at some point. A person can only take so much.

What current frustrations do you have and how can you solve them?

_____

_____

_____

_____

_____

_____

_____

_____

_____

_____

_____

_____

_____

_____

_____

_____

_____

_____

_____

_____

Chapter 7.

Detachment

Detaching from things that used to be of interest to you can occur. Maybe you are keeping more to yourself than usual and have not reached out to your family and friends. This can also include not taking care of yourself as much. A mother who has lost a child may end up detaching herself from her husband and he may feel that he has also lost his wife. Communicating your feelings becomes exceedingly difficult to express. However, you should reach out if you find yourself isolating too much. Try to talk to a friend and initiate a conversation or find a grief group on social media. What are some outlets you have or ideas for reaching out? Maybe try a creative outlet, such as music, art, or writing.

_____

_____

_____

_____

_____

_____

_____

_____

_____

_____

_____

_____

_____

_____

_____

_____

_____

_____

_____

_____

_____

_____

_____

_____

_____

Chapter 8.

Sorrow

Sorrow is sadness. You feel empty in your heart. You might feel numb and can't cry. Your world has been torn apart and you don't have direction. You may cry unexpectedly, hide in your house, and neglect yourself. Eating is a chore, or you turn to food to fill the void. Several physical symptoms happen when we are in sorrow. The world does not seem as bright as before. You have a hard time imagining life can ever be normal again. This is a time when you should try to think about how you can do baby steps to take care of yourself. Drink several glasses of water, try to get an extra hour or two of sleep, and eat solid foods. Build your energy back up.

What steps can you take to soothe your sorrow?

_____
_____
_____
_____
_____
_____
_____
_____
_____
_____
_____
_____
_____
_____
_____
_____
_____
_____
_____
_____
_____

Chapter 9.

Realization

In this stage you are starting to realize that your loved one is not coming back. Life is different now and you've managed to make it day by day. You find ways to do things in memory of them and hold them close to you. You are carrying on with life and making some progress that you never thought you were capable of in the beginning.

What progress have you made? List things you have done.

_____

_____

_____

_____

_____

_____

_____

_____

_____

_____

_____

_____

_____

_____

_____

_____

_____

_____

_____

_____

Chapter 10.

Awakening

This is your new normal. Maybe you have connected with the things you enjoyed doing before the loss or discovered new things to do. You are adapting to life in a different way and starting to feel peace in your heart.

How different do you feel now versus a few months ago? Did you start a new routine?

_____

_____

_____

_____

_____

_____

_____

_____

_____

_____

_____

_____

_____

_____

_____

_____

_____

_____

_____

_____

_____

_____

_____

_____

Chapter 10.

Gratitude

Gratitude is appreciation for what you do have. This can be found in the gifts your loved ones left you. The biggest gift is the memories you shared. You incorporate him or her in your life as you move forward. Their spirit is with you on your journey towards the rest of your life. Perhaps you have made this your purpose for getting out of bed each day. You will always love and miss them, but you don't have that heavy sadness as often. It is not easy to feel grief and gratitude at the same time. This shift is one that can change your entire perspective on grief. When my grandfather died, I was very grief stricken, however, his life meant more to me than his death. If you have reached this point, congratulations! You are on the upward spiral.

Write about how you are living in honor of your loved one. How has their life superseded the pain of their death? What specifically are you grateful for as a result of having known them?

_____

_____

_____

_____

_____

_____

_____

_____

_____

_____

_____

_____

_____

_____

_____

_____

_____

_____

Chapter 12.

Is grief and suffering a choice?

This question has gotten me into a lot of trouble. Many people believe that grief is love and never goes away. They remain in emotional pain and suffer the rest of their lives. I think that it is caused by a self-limiting belief pattern they create. They have a ceiling to their healing that only goes so far up and closes them in. Every day they hold onto their loss possibly because they think if they don't feel it then they are leaving their loved one behind. This couldn't be further from the truth. Truth is that their loved one's energy is always present. You can carry them with you in everything you do. I will go so far as to say that grieving them for years can be a dishonor to their memory. They loved you and would not want you to stifle your life by holding on to their death. Regardless of the age of your loved one, they are no longer living in this physical world. If they were given another day, do you think they would cry? Or would they soak in every second of being alive again? You can choose to suffer from who you don't have in your life, or you can be grateful for the life they lived. This is a choice. I have spoken to several women who have lost young children and so many of them decide to carry on and actually find their purpose in life from the death. They do not want their child's memory to be shrouded in pain but that of love and happiness. You will always love and miss them, but you don't have to feel the raw pain of grief for the rest of your life.

How are you choosing to respond to your grief now, at this moment?

_____
_____
_____
_____
_____
_____
_____
_____
_____
_____
_____
_____
_____
_____
_____
_____
_____

Chapter 13.

Finding a purpose

Finding a purpose is key. This can be achieved by digging into the memory of who you lost. Remember every detail of their smiles, their smell, what they stood for as a person. Define the spirit that made them unique and incorporate it into your life, your personality and everyday positivity. We are only alive in memory after we depart. Keeping that memory alive keeps them alive. After realizing this it will become your reason for getting out of bed each day. Your reason for going forward. It is a beautiful quest to take on and write this book. I took all the grief, sadness and heartache and put it into an action plan. My aunt Linda passed away very suddenly, and I remember feeling disbelief. Two weeks later, I decided that her life was going to be meaningful, and I decided to find a way to honor her.

This is exactly the way she handled her grief too. So, I'm taking on how she would handle loss and moving forward. Using her memory as motivation to help others. Her life was a gift for me and I'm trying to give this gift to you. After a while, you will start to see a domino effect. If you help one person, everyone around them will be positively affected. Their family, friends, coworkers and soon a community. All by that one life and the drive of your purpose will flourish. Take a few moments to think about your loved one and find ideas that you can pull from them to fit into your life. This can create an entirely new life for you with renewed joy. When you find your purpose, you will feel it. It's not necessarily a life changing event but a good feeling that you are here for a reason.

Setting up a daily intention can help you find a purpose in each day. What purposes have you found for yourself that keep you moving forward each day?

_____
_____
_____
_____
_____
_____
_____
_____
_____
_____
_____
_____
_____
_____

Chapter 14.

Post Traumatic Growth

Trauma is a negative response to an adverse event. Just about every death there is a traumatic response that loops in our thoughts. Most people will replay how their loved one died repeatedly. It is our way of comprehending why they are gone. The chain of events is what we think about constantly. Even if the death was expected to happen.

Although, there are sudden horrific instances that can cause Post Traumatic Syndrome Disorder. This is when the surviving family cannot come to terms with the way the death occurred or witnessed it. For example, motor vehicle accidents and suicides lend themselves to this disorder. Whether you actually find the body or were in the vehicle, these types of deaths can easily lead to complicated grief. Complicated grief is grief that has several factors involved that hinder a person's healing process. Guilt, shame, and blame come to the forefront in complex situations. For deep trauma, I recommend seeing a grief therapist. There are many methods they can assist you with in therapy. Although, a Grief Coach can help you to move forward if you are stuck in one particular place in your grief and it would be determined by the initial contact as to which professional would be able to help you the most.

In working with clients who have trauma as an effect, the method I use is to tell them about post traumatic growth. This is a new psychological term that relates to people who have gone through a traumatic event and gain a greater appreciation for life. Even the most terrible experiences can end up over the years as becoming an opportunity for growth. The other day I was talking to a mother who lost her three year old daughter from an accident several years ago and she said that her daughter, in her short life, taught her amazing things about love and appreciation for life. She promised her that she would go on and continue to share that love with anyone she could. She was able to honor her daughter's memory in this beautiful way. It was evident to me that even as years had gone by, knowing her meant knowing her daughter as well.

Have you experienced growth?

_____
_____
_____
_____
_____
_____
_____
_____
_____
_____

Chapter 15.

Mindfulness

Learning mindfulness completely changed my life for the better. It is about being in the present moment at all times. Think about it, when we go back into the past and get caught up in the death, we feel sad and hopeless. If we jump into the future, it's full of plans and promises that we cannot keep. Right now, in this moment we are safe. Practicing mindfulness affects everything that you do. Eating in a mindful way teaches us to use all of your senses when preparing and eating food. Staying in the moment decreases anxiety significantly as you are not forecasting a negative outcome. You will begin to live life in the moment and notice things that you never paid attention to. A gentle breeze across your face, the soft fur on your pet, the smell of fresh air. Gratitude is given several times a day when you are in a state of mindfulness. You learn to let go of unnecessary attachments and give to others in the most thoughtful way. Meditation and breathing becomes essential to quiet and relax the mind. You love yourself and others in a spirited manner. Worry takes a back seat as you realize and accept that everything changes and is in perfect order.

Years ago, when I was extremely physically sick with a chronic illness I have, I was near death. I didn't recognize myself in the mirror anymore or even looking down at my own body. I thought, this isn't me. This isn't me. And it wasn't me. I realized that I am not my body, and I am an energy. I recall thinking about my life as I had lived it. Type A personality and always impatient, a workaholic. I thought about going out in my 20s and people I knew. Was I dying? Yes, I was, down to 65lbs and so weak that I couldn't hold my head up. Then it sort of hit me that life is a puzzle. So many pieces have to fit together to connect. We can't see the picture although every event, meeting, change, life and death is another piece. Fitting together perfectly. Even death is a piece, actually I believe it's the final piece when we zoom back and finally understand our individual picture. Since that occurrence in my life, I can't get in a hurry if my life depends on it. I take my time and notice everything much more clearly. Appreciating a bee on a flower in the spring and the glitter in the snow. My path led me to find mindfulness. My mother was very mindful in how she lived her life. I didn't know that when she was alive unfortunately. Although I understand now and just by taking in the now moments, I'm honoring her. This is how I found peace in my life and true love in my heart.

Take notice of something right now and write about it. Use your five senses.

Chapter 16.

Places we used to go

Like the song, there is always something there to remind me. Places hold a special place in our hearts. Tattooed in our memories and only special to us. This place for me is Williamsburg, Virginia, the place I called home. My grandparents retired there and bought a large ranch style home. Residing in the house were my grandparents and my aunt Linda. Although every member of my mother's side of the family lived there at some point. This was the place to be during the holidays. Cozy fire going, a ball game on TV, two Christmas trees sparkling and plastic candles in every window. This was home. Traveling there after a long drive in winter, it was such a warm embrace just to enter inside. After my mother died in 2007, I tried to make it there as often as I could to represent her so my grandparents didn't feel the magnitude of her not being there. I tried my best to be happy and get them smiling. Everything about the town is littered with memories of when I lived there. Old friends, restaurants, the city of Williamsburg itself decorated so beautifully for Christmas. This year the house is as gutted as I am right now. Mom, my grandmother, and Linda died in 2020, a couple of months apart. My two surviving aunts are trying to clean it out to sell it. The house is dark and cold and dead. I have no reason to go back to Virginia now. It's a ghost of my fondest memories and everyone I loved. I have no safe place to fall back to if I ever need a place to go. I have lived in Georgia since 2002. I am the current owner of the house that belonged to my ex-boyfriend. He willed it to me before he took his life. So, living here after 4 years, it is only starting to feel like my home. There are so many reminders here of him. Many I refuse to part with because I don't want to erase his memory all together. But after so many years I've learned that home is where the heart is and in my heart is exactly where my family is now. If you are experiencing this, please remember those places fondly and take mental photos of your memories and hold them close to you. They are indeed very special.

Write about a special place that isn't the same since your loss.

_____
_____
_____
_____
_____
_____
_____
_____
_____
_____
_____
_____
_____

Chapter 17.

The Afterlife

I don't think death is the end. Through the years I've heard over a hundred times the same story. When people are close to death, they see their loved ones that have died. They come to them in visions. This happened when my grandmother was dying. She saw her mother and grandmother and she was talking to them. After hearing this from so many people, I no longer question if this is real or not. A mother will appear to her dying daughter and help her transition into the afterlife. No, this doesn't happen to everyone, but it's happened enough times to get my attention. Following a death, people also see them in their dreams often. They seldom speak and it's common that when you notice it's them, they disappear. These are referred to as visitation dreams. They are different from a normal dream. I think that it's their way of letting us know that they are still around us. Many people seek out Mediums to try to get answers from their departed. There's a lot of facts given that nobody else would know about. For centuries there have been ghost sightings. Things moving, lights flickering, strange sounds and so on. I don't have all of the answers regarding what really happens to us after our body dies but the soul is tangible. If you've ever seen someone pass away, you can literally see it in their eyes that they have left their body. As a Funeral Director I would hear, they look good but not like themselves. That's because they aren't in the body anymore. Like a light, our souls, spirits, energy, simply transcend into another realm. Some call this the Astral Plane. There are changes that occur there as the spirit moves through the different planes. Many people believe that we are reincarnated and go on to learn in another life. This is where karma plays an important role in which direction the souls go. Heaven of course is beautiful, and a place believed to be the ultimate destination for us. It is where God serves us instead of us serving him while alive. Unless you believe in nothingness, which there is no proof of, then you will consider some kind of afterlife. We get signs that bring us comfort. A hummingbird, cardinal, butterflies or maybe a breeze out of nowhere. We also tend to be in nature when we receive signs. We are drawn closer to our loved ones when we are immersed in the beauty of nature. I believe this is also a way we can communicate with them. The next time you feel sad, go outside, and connect with your natural surroundings and you may very well get a clear sign that they are listening and watching you. I refuse to believe that death is the absolute end.

Have you had any special experiences, dreams or signs?

_____

_____

_____

_____

_____

_____

_____

Chapter 18.

Be their storyteller

Do you ever wonder, why wasn't it me? You were so close to your loved one. You knew them inside and out. Maybe your role is to be their storyteller, their legacy. How many years were you together? What was their daily routine? Their values? Belief systems? How can you explain to a stranger who they were and what they meant to you? Describe their personality to someone or just write it down so you always remember. Doing this again, preserves them in time and keeps them alive. I remember talking to my nephew about my mother. He was only about 8 years old when she passed and years later, I was making one of her recipes. While cooking I told him that she used to make it all the time and how she taught me how to cook. When he sat down and took the first bite, he appreciated it as if she made it for him. He always asks me to make it for him, even at age 22. I think it's because we were able to make the association between her love and kindness into the meal and it was presented in her honor. There are numerous ways to do this with your family, friends, and new additions to your life. My grandmother enjoyed gardening and took up container gardening. She decorated her patio with little statues and water features. She created an atmosphere of beautiful blooms for the butterflies and no area was without her touch. Every time I see a bright pink petunia I stop, and my mind goes right to her garden.

Most people have their "thing" that they enjoyed doing. Crossword puzzles, painting, cooking, working on cars, loving animals to name examples. Hone in on what reminds you of your loved one and teach it, even if you are the only one who enjoys it. This is telling their story.

Please share as many stories as possible! Have love in your heart as you reflect.

_____

_____

_____

_____

_____

_____

_____

_____

_____

_____

_____

Chapter 19.

Things you can do

Journaling is a great way to release your feelings. You can write your entry to your loved one and talk to them about your days. I recommend that you end each day on a positive note. The last section of the book is dedicated as a journal for you.

Write a letter to them about what your life has been like since they passed away. At the end of the letter think about 3 promises to make to them and set them as goals for yourself. Doing things in their memory will help you be more accountable for carrying them out.

A letter of self-compassion. Especially if you are a caregiver of the person. Show yourself some sympathy for everything you've done out of love for them and realize that you did everything possible to make their life easier. Give yourself a break from feeling that you did not do enough. At the end of the letter, write, I love you.

Here's an exercise that I call, I AM and He or She WAS. On a piece of paper draw a line through the middle horizontally. On the top write I AM, give yourself 2 minutes to write down all of your positive qualities. Then on the second half of the paper write either HE or SHE WAS and do the same thing writing about their qualities. When you are done you will notice similar traits but select 2 or 3 from your loved one that you can incorporate into your life. This helps you to keep them alive in memory and follow in their footsteps.

Chapter 20.

Daily Gratitude and Mindfulness

Each day I get a cup of coffee and go outside and take in each sip and look at my surroundings. Fresh air, animals running around, and birds singing. I give heartfelt gratitude for at least 3 things in my life each day. Always keep in mind what you do have instead of what you don't have. Ground yourself in the present moment and breathe deeply into your belly and let the air fill your lungs as exhale. Or you can breathe deeply into your heart and let it open up. We store grief in different areas of our body. You can do a body scan by laying down on your back and scanning your body with your hand to find where you have the most tension. Once you discover the area, breathe deep with your hand over the area. As you inhale pull your hand away a few inches as though you are gently pulling the tension away from your body. Completely relaxed.

Chapter 20.

Meditation

The natural cycle for meditation when you begin is you focus, wander, notice that you are wandering and guide yourself back to focusing. The mind thinks just as the heart beats so it's hard to control your thoughts. After time you will be able to shut out the world and concentrate more on your breath. For some people guided meditation works, some enjoy soft music and incense or everything quiet. Try 5 minutes in the beginning and work up to 10 minutes. You may do this whenever you feel it's needed or as often as necessary for you.

Heart Activation Meditation

This is my favorite and most powerful meditation. Your heart has been broken, shattered, closed off. It is especially important to allow yourself to mend and open your heart. The most important part of this meditation is getting the breathing right. I like to do it laying on my back. You will close your mouth and loosen your abdominal muscles. This is a continuous breath. Inhale through your nose into your belly as you inhale and keep inhaling slowly as the air fills your lungs and heart. When the air is in the back of your throat, you will exhale through the nose. Do this nice and slow but never holding your breath. Your head will begin to feel a little tingly and very relaxed. Once you feel very calm and good, about five minutes in, close your eyes and imagine your heart blossoming open like a giant red rose. Feel your heart opening and allow love and gratitude to flow through your body. Think about everything you love and are grateful for. You will be in a state of bliss, and you may keep yourself there for as long as you wish. That breathing exercise is also helpful during times of anxiety or whenever you want to calm yourself. How do you feel after doing this meditation?

_____

_____

_____

_____

_____

_____

_____

_____

_____

_____

_____

_____

The Love and Kindness Meditation

This is a good meditation for self-compassion, empathy, and forgiveness. Place your hand on your heart. Close your eyes and say to yourself.

May I be happy,

May I be healthy,

May I live in peace.

Think about someone you love unconditionally and say,

May them be happy,

May them be healthy,

May them live in peace.

Think of someone you have hostile feelings for and say,

May them be happy,

May them be healthy,

May them live in peace.

The Kind Hands Meditation

Look at your hands and think of all the loving and caring actions you have done with them. You may have taken care of your loved one, you may have helped bathe another, held a baby, wrapped your arms around someone in an embrace, held another's hand, brushed a child's hair. Think about your kind hands and how you expressed love with them. Take a moment and write about your kind hands.

_____

_____

_____

_____

_____

_____

_____

_____

_____

_____

_____

_____

_____

_____

_____

_____

_____

_____

_____

_____

_____

_____

_____

_____

A Safe Place Meditation

Close your eyes and take nice deep breaths and imagine the perfect place for you. It could be on a beach, in a cabin on a mountain with snow, any place that you can dream up. Visualize the atmosphere. Use all of your senses to fully imagine you are here. This is your secret getaway and safe place. Perhaps your loved one is there with you, and this is a secret meet up that only belongs to you. Write in detail about your safe place.

Ho'oponopono Mantra

Ho'oponopono is an old Hawaiian mantra that has helped thousands of people learn to love themselves. It is quite simple and powerful. You will say this to yourself and for others. It expresses self-compassion, forgiveness, love, and gratitude. I often add something to the end of each line. Here it is:

I'm Sorry,

I Forgive you,

I Love you,

Thank you.

Chapter 22.

The Firsts

The firsts are extremely difficult. The first birthday, anniversary, Thanksgiving, and holidays. Not only are they not here but we are without their love for us. That is a big gap. Some ideas for getting through these times can be as follows.

Birthdays- Get a birthday card for them and have everyone write a special note. Make a photo album. Play their favorite music and prepare a nice gathering of friends at a restaurant. Make a post on social media requesting friends to share funny stories, pictures and memories.

Anniversary- Buy flowers or plant a unique garden or tree. Be creative about the symbol for that year of marriage. For example, 25 years is silver, have a piece of jewelry made of silver. Have a balloon release if it is the anniversary of their passing.

Thanksgiving- A time of gratitude, have everyone pitch in with a dish to make it easier for you. Go around the table and share a funny memory of your loved one.

The holidays-Have a smaller tree decorated just in honor of your loved one, Make it special and colorful. A client of mine was dreading Christmas because it was his late wife's favorite holiday. It happened that she had a large collection of angels. I suggested decorating the house in an angelic snowy wonderland and he got extremely excited and did a wonderful job.

I hope this book has given you some guidance and helped coach you through the grieving process. It is easy to drift into a downward spiral of despair. However, with help you can move forth in your loss up the upward spiral of gratitude for them being in our life. The next pages are dedicated for journaling. As you write about your journey, please try to end each entry on a positive note if you can. One day you will look back and see how far you have come. Thank you.

Journal

Made in the USA
Las Vegas, NV
20 September 2021